W9-DEI-438

Funny Bone Jokes

Animal JOKES to Tickle Your FUNNY BONE

Michele C. Hollow

Summit Free Public Library

Enslow Elementary
an imprint of
Enslow Publishers, Inc.
40 Industrial Road
Box 398
Berkeley Heights, NJ 07922
USA

http://www.enslow.com

To Steven, for making me laugh.
Love, Michele

Enslow Elementary, an imprint of Enslow Publishers, Inc.

Enslow Elementary® is a registered trademark of Enslow Publishers, Inc.

Copyright © 2011 by Michele C. Hollow.

Library of Congress Cataloging-in-Publication Data

Hollow, Michele C.
   Animal jokes to tickle your funny bone / Michele C. Hollow.
      p. cm. — (Funny bone jokes)
   Includes bibliographical references and index.
   Summary: "Includes jokes, limericks, knock knock jokes, tongue twisters, and fun facts about cats, dogs, ocean animals, jungle animals, farm animals, and more, and describes how to write your own joke book"—Provided by publisher.
   ISBN 978-0-7660-3544-7
   1. Animals—Juvenile humor. I. Title.
PN6231.A5H65 2010
818'.602—dc22

                              2010004189

ePUB ISBN 978-1-4645-0315-3
PDF ISBN 978-1-4646-0315-0

Printed in the United States of America

122011 Lake Book Manufacturing, Inc., Melrose Park, IL

10 9 8 7 6 5 4 3 2

To Our Readers: We have done our best to make sure all Internet Addresses in this book were active and appropriate when we went to press. However, the author and the publisher have no control over and assume no liability for the material available on those Internet sites or on other Web sites they may link to. Any comments or suggestions can be sent by e-mail to comments@enslow.com or to the address on the back cover.

Every effort has been made to locate all copyright holders of material used in this book. If any errors or omissions have occurred, corrections will be made in future editions of this book.

♻ Enslow Publishers, Inc., is committed to printing our books on recycled paper. The paper in every book contains 10% to 30% post-consumer waste (PCW). The cover board on the outside of each book contains 100% PCW. Our goal is to do our part to help young people and the environment too!

Illustration Credits: All clip art from © Clipart.com, a division of Getty Images, and photos on pp. 5, 6, 17, 18, 20, 23, 34, 36; Shutterstock, pp. 9, 10, 12, 14, 25, 27, 29, 32, 38, 40, 42, 45.

Cover Illustration: All clip art from © Clipart.com, a division of Getty Images.

Contents

1	Cats	4
2	Dogs	8
3	Birds	12
4	Ocean Animals	16
5	Chickens	20

6	Jungle Animals	25
7	Farm Animals	29
8	Snakes	33
9	Insects	37
10	Bears	41

Write Your Own Joke Book	46
Read More	47
Index	48

Cats

What do you call a cat who eats lemons?

A sourpuss!

What do you call a cat who's joined the Red Cross?

A first-aid kit!

Knock, Knock!

Who's there?

Neil.

Neil who?

Neil down and pet this cat!

How can you tell if your cat has been using your computer?

Your mouse has teeth marks on it.

What is a French cat's favorite pudding?

Chocolate mousse!

There was a fat cat on a mat
Who liked to chase mice named Pat.
He chased them around
And fell on the ground
And smashed them until they were flat!

DID YOU KNOW THAT cats are the number ONE pet in the United States?

According to the American Veterinary Medical Association, there are more than 81,721,000 cats living in the United States. Cats make great pets. They are friendly and love to play. Indoor cats can live to 20-plus years.

IT'S TRUE.

Why does everyone love cats?

They're purr-fect!

The crooked cat goes down the crooked stairs crookedly.

Each time you see this squiggly box, it is a tongue twister! Try saying it five times fast!

How do cats buy things?

From a cat-alogue!

What kind of cat loves to bowl?

An alley cat.

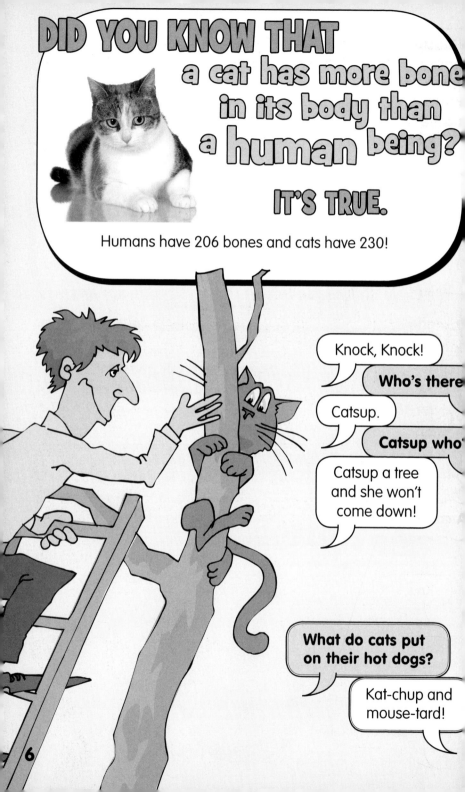

black-and-white kitten called Spot
aused trouble, all day quite a lot,
He fell down the stairs,
cratched all of the chairs,
nd he loved the attention he got.

What is a cat's favorite color?

Purr-ple!

A curious cream-colored cat crept into a cave.

What is a limerick?

Limericks are five-line verses that have a definite pattern. The first two and last lines rhyme and the third and fourth lines rhyme. Listen to this limerick and hear the beat. "An artistic young man named Bo. To an art class decided to go. The teacher said, 'not right. Your page is all white.' Bo said, 'it's a polar bear in the snow.'"

calico cat caught a colorful canary.

Knock, Knock!

Who's there?

Claws.

Claws who?

Claws the door behind us!

7

2 Dogs

Why do dogs wag their tails?

Because no one else will do it for them.

Why do dogs bury bones in the ground?

Because they can't bury them in trees!

Dad's dogs dig delicious donuts.

What is a joke?

Everyone has heard "Why did the chicken cross the road?" It is one of the oldest and most familiar jokes around. The most common answer is "to get to the other side." However, chickens crossing the road have led to many jokes filled with various answers. Jokes make us laugh.

What do you get if you cross a sheepdog with a rose?

A collie-flower!

FUN FACTS

The world's heaviest and longest dog was an Old English mastiff named Zorba. In 1989, Zorba weighed 343 pounds and was 8 feet 3 inches long from nose to tail!

IT'S TRUE.

Why did the snowman call his dog Frost?

Because frost bites!

What kind of dog does Dracula have?

A bloodhound!

Knock, Knock!

Who's there?

Arthur.

Arthur who?

Arthur any more dogs out there?

Dina's dog Daisy digs in dirt.

What do you get if you cross a giraffe with a dog?

An animal that barks at low-flying aircraft!

Knock, Knock!

Who's there?

Ken.

Ken who?

Ken I bring my dog inside?

Why do dogs run in circles?

Because it's hard to run in squares!

DID YOU KNOW THAT all dogs are related to the Wolf?

Scientists believe that friendship between dogs and people began more than 14,000 years ago. This friendship began when humans tried to tame wolf pups by giving them food. Over the centuries, humans have used dogs as hunters and watchdogs.

IT'S TRUE.

There was a Young Lady of Ryde,
Whose shoestrings were seldom untied;
She purchased some clogs,
and some small spotty dogs,
And frequently walked about Ryde.

Dave's dog Doogie digs
for dinosaur bones.

What do you get if you
cross a cocker spaniel, a
poodle, and a rooster?

Cockerpoodledoo!

Why did the poor
dog chase his own tail?

He was trying to make
both ends meet!

Knock, Knock!

Who's there?

Sarah.

Sarah who?

Sarah dog in
there with you?

There once was a dog named Buffy
Her fur was rather quite fluffy
Her neighbor next door
Was a beagle named Thor
Together they had a litter of puppies.

3 Birds

What happens when ducks fly upside down?

They quack up!

What bird is always sad?

The blue jay

Seagulls sit on seashells on the seashore.

What does a duck like to eat with soup?

Quackers.

DID YOU KNOW THAT

birds build their nests almost everywhere?

IT'S TRUE.

They build their nests on the ground and on the highest treetops. The belted kingfisher builds its nest in the bank of a river or creek. Grebes build floating nests on water.

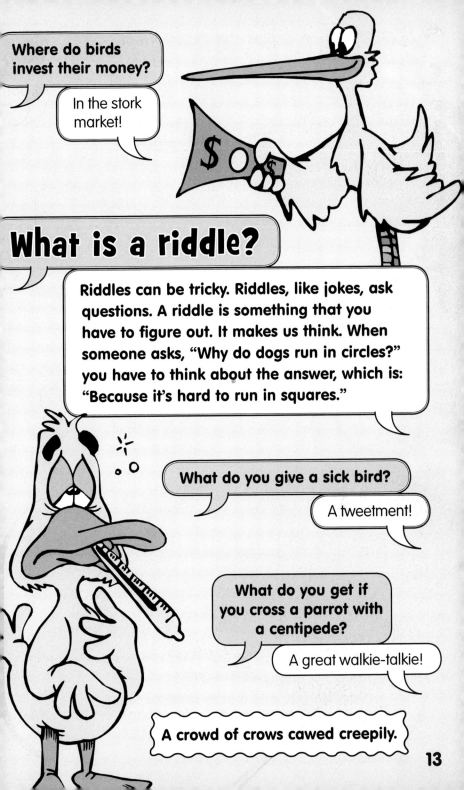

Where do birds invest their money?

In the stork market!

What is a riddle?

Riddles can be tricky. Riddles, like jokes, ask questions. A riddle is something that you have to figure out. It makes us think. When someone asks, "Why do dogs run in circles?" you have to think about the answer, which is: "Because it's hard to run in squares."

What do you give a sick bird?

A tweetment!

What do you get if you cross a parrot with a centipede?

A great walkie-talkie!

A crowd of crows cawed creepily.

DID YOU KNOW THAT the largest bird in the world is the ostrich?

This bird can weigh up to 300 pounds. Being the largest bird, it makes sense that the ostrich would lay the biggest eggs—measuring six to eight inches long.

IT'S TRUE.

Why do seagulls live near the sea?

Because if they lived near the bay, they would be called bagels.

There was a young lady whose bonnet Came untied when the birds sat upon it; But she said, "I don't care! All the birds in the air Are welcome to sit on my bonnet!"

What do you call a very rude bird?

A mockingbird!

Ocean Animals

What fish is great for playing a piano?

A tune-a-fish

Why didn't the lobster share his toys?

He was too shellfish.

What fish makes the best sandwiches?

A peanut butter and jellyfish.

Why do penguins eat fish?

Because donuts get soggy.

What do you call a fish with no eyes?

FSH.

What did one octopus say to the other?

I want to hold your hand, hand, hand, hand, hand, hand, hand, hand.

DID YOU KNOW THAT fish can get dirty?

IT'S TRUE.

We tend to think of fish swimming all day and night in the water keeping clean. After all, don't we feel clean when we are taking a bath? Well, fish can have tiny animals living on their scales. If these tiny animals aren't cleaned, the fish can get sick.

Why are fish so smart?

Because they live in schools.

What fish has the most value?

Goldfish.

Why did the shark wear a tuxedo?

He was dressed to kill.

Knock, Knock!

Who's there?

Tuna.

Tuna who?

Tuna piano and it'll sound better!

DID YOU KNOW THAT seahorses are a type of fish?

They don't look like a typical fish. They are named seahorses because their long noses and bodies are shaped like a horse. The male seahorse is the one who gives birth to the babies. They can have up to 100 babies at a time!

IT'S TRUE.

Knock, Knock!

Who's there?

Whale.

Whale who?

Whale will you let me in or won't you?

Phillip finds fishy freckled fishes.

There was an old person of Dundalk,
Who tried to teach fishes to walk;
When they tumbled down dead,
He grew weary, and said,
"I had better go back to Dundalk!"

What is a tongue twister?

Tongue twisters all have a bit of music in them. Just listen to yourself as you say, "A big brown cow bought a bunch of bananas." Hear the rhythm in that tongue twister? It's fun to say even though you will feel like your tongue is tied up—especially if you say it very fast.

Turtles take time to travel.

There was an old person of Ickley,
Who could not abide to ride quickly;
He rode to Karnak
On a tortoise's back,
That moony old person of Ickley.

5 Chickens

What do you call a crazy chicken?

A cuckoo cluck!

Why did the dinosaur cross the road?

Because chickens weren't born yet.

Why did the horse cross the road?

Because the chicken needed a day off.

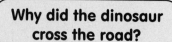 **DID YOU KNOW THAT** the chicken is the closest living relative of the *Tyrannosaurus rex*?

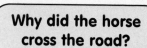

IT'S TRUE. Scientists compared and studied old dinosaur bones and new chicken bones. They discovered similar material found in each, making the chicken and *Tyrannosaurus rex* distant cousins. The link between chickens and dinosaurs is an exciting one because scientists are using the material they have found to study human illness.

Why did the chewing gum cross the road?

Because it was stuck to the chicken!

What do you call a rooster who wakes you up at the same time every morning?

An alarm cluck!

What is a knock knock joke?

Knock knock jokes are back-and-forth questions and answers. You start by saying: "Knock, knock!"

Someone answers: "Who's there?" Then you reply, a friend answers, and you end it.

Here's an example: "Knock, knock!" "Who's there?" "Alpaca." "Alpaca who?" "Alpaca the trunk, you pack-a the suitcase." These type of knock knock jokes are called puns or play on words.

Why did the chicken cross the basketball court?

He heard the referee calling fowls.

A man has to get a fox, a chicken, and a sack of corn across a river. He has a rowboat, and it can only carry him and one other thing. If the fox and the chicken are left together, the fox will eat the chicken. If the chicken and the corn are left together, the chicken will eat the corn. How does the man do it?

Man carries the chicken. Man leaves the chicken and comes back. Man gets fox. Man leaves fox and gets chicken. Man leaves chicken and gets corn. Man leaves fox and corn to get chicken. Man gets chicken.

Knock, Knock!

Who's there?

Megan, Elise, and Chicken.

Megan, Elise, and Chicken who?

He is Megan, Elise, and Chicken it twice, going to find out who's naughty and nice.

Knock, Knock!

Who's there?

Chicken.

Chicken who?

Just chicken out the doorbell.

DID YOU KNOW THAT there are more chickens on earth than there are humans?

IT'S TRUE.

China has the most people in the world, and also the most chickens. There are more than 3 billion chickens in China! The United States has only 450 million chickens.

Six sick chicks with sticks

Why does a chicken coop have two doors?

Because if it had four doors it would be a chicken sedan!

A man who ate chickens once said:
"I once ate a chicken not dead.
It clucked in my belly
As I watched the telly,
And it clucked as I lay in my bed."

What happened to the chicken whose feathers were all pointing the wrong way?

She was tickled to death!

Knock, Knock!

Who's there?

Cheese.

Cheese who?

Cheese no spring chicken.

Chirping chickens chatter while chomping on cherries.

There was an old man with a beard.
What happened was what he had feared.
Two roosters and a crow,
Three ravens, don't you know,
Had all made nests in his beard.

Jungle Animals

Why do elephants never forget?

Because nobody ever tells them anything!

Happy hippo Hal hiccups.

What do you get if you cross a fish with an elephant?

Swimming trunks!

DID YOU KNOW THAT there are more than 100 different types of monkeys?

Monkeys are found in Africa, Asia, Mexico, Central America, and South America. Howler monkeys can be found in the Amazon rain forest in Brazil.

IT'S TRUE.

DID YOU KNOW THAT elephants are the largest land animals in the world?

There are two kinds of elephants—African and Asian. You can easily tell them apart because African elephants are bigger and taller than Asian elephants. Asian elephants have smaller ears and shorter tusks than African elephants. Since both African and Asian elephants are so big, they spend a lot of time eating—twenty hours a day!

IT'S TRUE.

When is a well-dressed lion like a weed?

When he's a dandelion (dandy lion).

Knock, Knock!

Who's there?

Gorilla.

Gorilla who?

Gorilla me a hamburger, I'm hungry.

Why is it hard to play cards in the jungle?

There are too many cheetahs.

Monkeys make marshmallow milkshakes.

A boa constrictor named Larry
was fully unable to carry.
No arms had the snake,
so for convenience's sake,
an octopus Larry did marry.

Knock, Knock!

Who's there?

Elsie.

Elsie, who?

Elsie you later, alligator.

What kind of snake is good at math?

An adder.

There was a young lady from Niger,
Who smiled as she rode on a tiger.
After the ride
She was inside,
And the smile was on the face of the tiger.

28

Farm Animals

What did the judge say when the skunk walked in the courtroom?

Odor in the court!

What do you get when you cross a rooster with a duck?

You get woken up by the quack of dawn.

A skunk sat on a stump.

DID YOU KNOW THAT there are six different types of COWS?

The different kinds of cows include: Holsteins, which are the most common, and Guernseys, Jerseys, Brown Swiss, Ayrshires, and Milking Shorthorns. Holsteins are large with black-and-white patterns on their fur. No two cows look alike. Each one has a different pattern.

IT'S TRUE.

There was an Old Person whose habits,
Induced him to feed upon rabbits;
When he'd eaten eighteen,
He turned perfectly green,
Upon which he gave up those habits.

Knock, Knock!

Who's there?

Goat.

Goat who?

Goat to the door and find out!

What is a rabbit's favorite dance style?

Hip-Hop!

Why did the pony have to gargle?

Because it was a little horse

There was a young girl of Greenwich,
Whose clothes were covered with spinach;
But a large spotted calf
Bit her dress in half,
Which scared that young girl of Greenwich.

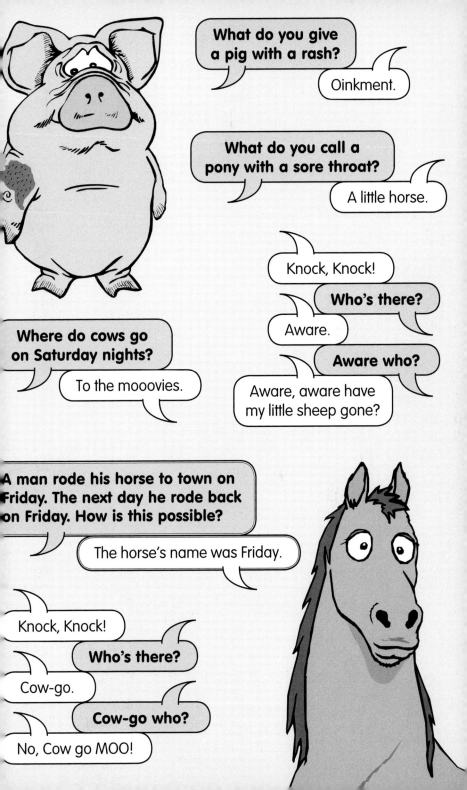

DID YOU KNOW THAT sheep have good memories?

Sheep can recognize at least fifty different sheep and ten human faces for more than two years. They can even recognize positive or negative emotions—and respond to pictures of friendly faces.

IT'S TRUE.

Harry the hare has heaps of fun hopping.

What did the horse say when it fell?

I've fallen and I can't giddyup!

Cows and crows chomp on corn.

How do you know that carrots are good for your eyesight?

Well, have you ever seen a rabbit wearing glasses?

Snakes

What should a snake yell if it wants to scare a ghost?

Boa!

Knock, Knock!

Who's there?

Snake.

Snake who?

Snake me out to the ball game.

What is a snake's favorite subject?

Hissstory.

Where do snakes go to have fun?

The boa-ling alley.

Sally's snake Sara squiggles and squirms.

When I went out to my garden on Monday,
I caught a big snake that was gray.
I tried and I tried,
To keep him inside,
Yet he escaped and slithered away.

Karl's cobra caught a cold.

What do snakes put on their kitchen floors?

Rep-tiles.

What does a well-dressed snake wear?

A boa tie.

How do you measure a snake?

In inches, since they don't have any feet.

They said, "What a marvelous dance!
Look at him jump and prance!"
He replied, "No applause,
It is only because
A snake is up the leg of my pants!"

What did the naughty little cobra say to his brother?

Don't be a rattletail.

DID YOU KNOW THAT snakes shed their skins when they grow?

IT'S TRUE.

Snakes and other reptiles shed their skins between four and eight times a year. A snake usually sheds its skin in one piece. The loose skin feels a bit like very thin wax paper. The shedding starts around the head and moves down the body. Snakes that are covered in old skin slowly move next to rough objects. By sliding by a rough object, the snake can slide out of its old skin.

Reptiles rock, rattle, and roll.

Knock, Knock!

Who's there?

Snakeskin.

Snakeskin who?

Snakes-kin bite, but we'd rather run away.

Sam's snake sneezed while sleeping.

Insects 9

What goes zzub, zzub?

A bee flying backwards!

How do bees get to school?

By school buzz!

Why do bees buzz?

Because they can't whistle!

Ants ate apples and avocados.

There was an Old Man in a tree,
Who was horribly bored by a Bee;
When they said, "Does it buzz?"
He replied, "Yes, it does!"
"It's a regular brute of a Bee!"

Knock, Knock!

Who's there?

Ants.

Ants who?

Ants in your pants will make you dance.

37

DID YOU KNOW THAT three out of four creatures on earth are bugs?

For every person, there are a million ants. Scientists have identified about one million different types of bugs, and these are the bugs we know about. There are several unknown types of bugs living on this planet. The oldest known fossils of insects date back to 400 million years ago. They have been around before the dinosaurs.

IT'S TRUE.

What is worse than an alligator with a toothache?

A centipede with athlete's foot.

Why was the centipede late?

Because he was playing "This Little Piggy" with his baby brother!

Bertie's bees buzz and burp.

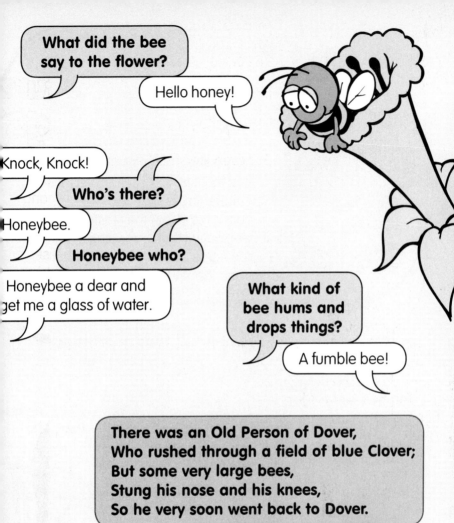

What did the bee say to the flower?

Hello honey!

Knock, Knock!

Who's there?

Honeybee.

Honeybee who?

Honeybee a dear and get me a glass of water.

What kind of bee hums and drops things?

A fumble bee!

There was an Old Person of Dover,
Who rushed through a field of blue Clover;
But some very large bees,
Stung his nose and his knees,
So he very soon went back to Dover.

What did one bea say to the other after a night out?

Shall we walk home or take a dog?

Frida's fly flew, flipped, and fell.

DID YOU KNOW THAT butterflies are cold-blooded animals?

They will not fly unless the weather is at least 50 degrees Fahrenheit. Another interesting fact about butterflies is that they taste with their feet, not with their mouths. They have tiny nerve endings on their feet that allow them to taste their food.

IT'S TRUE.

Knock, Knock!

Who's there?

Chimney.

Chimney who?

Chimney cricket! Have you seen Pinocchio?

How do you spot a modern spider?

He doesn't have a web, he has a Web site!

What are the cleverest bees?

Spelling bees!

DID YOU KNOW THAT there are eight different types of bears in the world?

IT'S TRUE.

The American black bear lives in North America. The brown bear lives in Canada, Alaska, and northern Eurasia. Polar bears, the largest species of bear, live in areas that border the Arctic Circle. Pandas are found in the central mountains of China. The Asiatic black bear lives in southern and eastern Asia. Sloth bears are found in tropical forests of India, Sri Lanka, and Nepal. The speckled bear lives in forests in South America. The sun bear lives in Malaysia and is one of the smallest types of bears.

Why are teddy bears never hungry?

Because they are always stuffed.

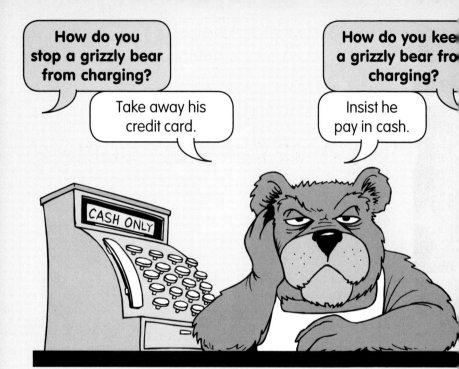

How do you stop a grizzly bear from charging?

Take away his credit card.

How do you kee[p] a grizzly bear fro[m] charging?

Insist he pay in cash.

The big black bear busily ate a batch of bagels, bananas, and blintzes.

What animal do you look like when you get into the tub?

A little bear (bare).

There once was a bear with no hair.
He felt cold and oh so bare.
He tried to cover his toes,
His fingers and nose.
Alas, that poor bear felt despair.

DID YOU KNOW THAT panda bears WEREN'T always thought to be part of the bear family?

For years, scientists thought giant pandas were related to raccoons. Scientists studied giant pandas and found that they are indeed bears. Other than both having a "mask" around the eyes, giant pandas and raccoons don't look alike.

IT'S TRUE.

What did the bear say after he saw campers in sleeping bags?

Yum, sandwiches.

Write Your Own Joke Book

HERE'S WHAT YOU WILL NEED:

- paper
- colored pencils, pens, or markers
- colorful folder
- staple gun with staples

DIRECTIONS:

1. Pick a topic. This book happens to be about animals. Once you have chosen your topic, write a table of contents.

2. Have one chapter for jokes/knock knock jokes, one for riddles, one for tongue twisters, and one for limericks.

3. Start writing your jokes, riddles, tongue twisters, and limericks. Put the jokes in the joke chapter, the riddles in the riddles chapter, and so on.

4. You can write each joke in a different color or decorate with pictures on each page.

5. Decorate the folder as you wish. This will be the cover of the book. Be sure to put your name on it.

6. Place the contents inside the folder and staple everything together down the side so it opens like a book.

Read More

Books

Chmielewski, Gary. *The Animal Zone: Jokes, Riddles, Tongue Twisters, and "Daffynitions."* Chicago, Ill.: Norwood House Press, 2008.

Horsfall, Jacqueline. *Joke and Riddle Ballyhoo*. New York: Sterling, 2005.

Myers, Janet Nuzum. *Critter Jokes and Riddles*. New York: Sterling, 2007.

Phillips, Bob. *Awesome Knock Knock Jokes for Kids*. Eugene, Ore.: Harvest House Publishers, 2006.

Internet Addresses

Jokes for Kids
<**http://www.activityvillage.co.uk/kids_jokes.htm**>

NIEHS Kids' Pages: Jokes, Humor, and Trivia
<**http://kids.niehs.nih.gov/jokes.htm**>

Index

A
ants, 37, 38

B
beagle, 11
bears, 41–45
bees, 37, 38, 39, 40
birds, 12–15

C
cats, 4–7
chickens, 20–24
cows, 19, 29, 30, 31

D
dogs, 8–11
ducks, 12, 15, 29

E
elephants, 25, 26, 27

F
farm animals, 29–32
fish and ocean animals, 16–19

G
goldfish, 17

H
hippopotamus, 25, 26

I
insects, 37–40

J
jungle animals, 25–28

L
lion, 26, 27

M
mockingbird, 14
monkeys, 25, 28

O
Old English mastiff, 9
ostrich, 14

P
penguins, 16
pigs, 31, 43

R
rabbits, 30, 32

S
seahorse, 18
sheep, 32
skunk, 29
snakes, 33–36
stork, 13

T
Tyrannosaurus rex, 20

W
whale, 18
wolf, 10